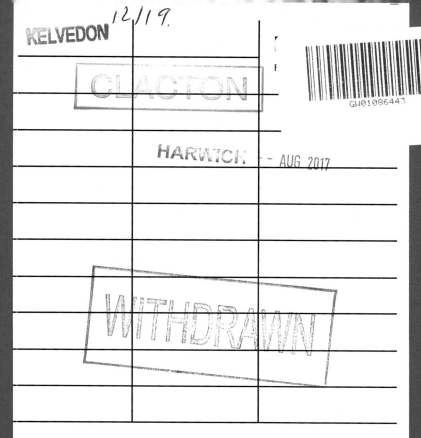

Please return this book on or before the date shown above. To renew go to www.essex.gov.uk/libraries, ring 0845 603 7628 or go to any Essex library.

Essex County Council

THE
MIDDLE
AGES

Usborne Quicklinks

The Usborne Quicklinks Website is packed with thousands of links to all the best websites on the internet. The websites include information, video clips, sounds, games and animations that support and enhance the information in Usborne internet-linked books.

To visit the recommended websites for this book, go to the Usborne Quicklinks Website at **www.usborne-quicklinks.com** and enter the keywords **History of Britain**, then click on **The Middle Ages**.

When using the internet please follow the internet safety guidelines displayed on the Usborne Quicklinks Website. The recommended websites in Usborne Quicklinks are regularly reviewed and updated, but Usborne Publishing Ltd. is not responsible for the content or availability of any website other than its own. We recommend that children are supervised while using the internet.

USBORNE HISTORY OF BRITAIN

THE
MIDDLE
AGES

Kate Davies, Conrad Mason & Dr. Abigail Wheatley

Illustrated by Ian McNee & Giacinto Gaudenzi

Designed by Anna Gould, Stephen Moncrieff
& Stephen Wright

Edited by Ruth Brocklehurst & Jane Chisholm

Consultant: Prof. Christopher Dyer, University of Leicester

Contents

Medieval Britain

In 1066, the Normans invaded and conquered England, marking the start of a new era. Along with their ruthless fighters, the new Norman kings brought French culture and language, binding England and France with strong political ties that lasted for several centuries. These changes had their effects on life in Wales, Ireland and Scotland too.

But kings didn't have it all their own way. Changes in technology, vast wars and terrible diseases all had their impact on ordinary people, who repeatedly rose up to express their anger and frustration. It was the people, as much as their leaders, who changed the course of history in medieval Britain.

HIC EXEVNT: CABAL

The Bayeux Tapestry

The Bayeux Tapestry is a huge embroidered cloth that tells the story of the Norman conquest of England, in pictures. It's about 50cm (20 inches) wide and over 70m (230ft) long.

It was made for the Normans shortly after 1066, by English women. Because it was designed for the winning side to celebrate their victory, it may not be entirely truthful.

The Norman Conquest

One bright October morning in 1066, near Hastings on the English south coast, two armies – the English and the Norman – were poised, ready to fight. The battle that followed was decisive, as it brought in a whole new line of rulers from France.

A few months earlier, Edward the Confessor, King of England, had died suddenly, leaving no heirs. There were three strong contenders for the throne: Harold Godwinson, a powerful English lord; Harald Hardrada, King of Norway; and William, Duke of Normandy, in France. The King's council of chief advisers – known as the Witan – wanted to settle the matter as quickly as possible.

So when Harold claimed that, on his deathbed, Edward had named him as his heir, they had him crowned the very next day.

From the outset, Harold was expecting trouble from his rivals – especially William. So he positioned an army all along the south coast, ready to defend against an attack from Normandy.

DENAVIBVS: ET hIC: MILITES: FESTINA VERY NT: hES

A waiting game

They waited all summer, but nothing happened. The army was just about to disband when shocking news came – Hardrada had invaded northern England. At once, Harold and his army charged north, moving so quickly they were able to surprise the enemy. At the Battle of Stamford Bridge, in Yorkshire, the Norwegians fought fiercely, but the English defeated them, decimating their troops and killing Hardrada.

Normans invade

But the English had barely started celebrating when yet more disastrous news arrived. William and his army had crossed the English Channel with a huge fleet. They had invaded southern England, and set up camp at Hastings. Exhausted from the battle, Harold mustered his troops, and sped back south to meet the invasion force.

This is a section of the Bayeux Tapestry. It shows the Normans landing near Hastings, and unloading their horses. The Normans' expertise in fighting on horseback would give them a crucial advantage against the English.

The Bayeux Tapestry depicts a comet that appeared in 1066. Many people thought it was a warning of terrible things to come.

7

The Battle of Hastings

> "Look, I am here, and with the grace of God I will win the day!"

William is said to have spoken these words during the battle, when gossip spread that he had been killed. He pushed back his helmet, crying out to his men to encourage them and to prove that he was alive.

This photograph shows a reenactment of the Battle of Hastings.

The two armies came face to face near Hastings, on October 14, 1066. It was to be a hard-fought battle. William's men had better training and equipment. They included archers and horsemen. Harold's soldiers were exhausted from fighting in the north only days earlier. But they held a strong position at the top of a hill, where they formed a wall with their shields, which the Norman soldiers found impossible to penetrate.

The armies became locked in a stalemate, until William came up with a plan that changed the course of the battle. He ordered his army to pretend to run away. When some of the English soldiers gave chase, the Normans turned around, slaughtering the English and riding triumphantly through the front line.

As soon as they had broken through the English ranks, the Normans easily overcame Harold's troops. Harold himself was killed, and the Normans declared a victory.

But the Battle of Hastings didn't mark the end of the Norman Conquest. William and his troops faced strong resistance from English lords as they advanced from Hastings to London for his coronation on Christmas Day, 1066. Even then, William was far from secure in his position and his soldiers remained on their guard. During the ceremony, they heard the sound of cheers from nearby houses, and mistook it for the start of a riot. They panicked, and set the houses on fire. Eyewitnesses reported that William was shaking with fear as the crown was put on his head.

A bloody battle

No one knows exactly how Harold was killed, but the Bayeux Tapestry shows him with an arrow in his eye, and being hacked from his horse by a Norman knight.

After his victory, William built an abbey named Battle as a memorial to the dead. The altar is positioned on the spot where Harold is said to have been killed.

Knights

One of the things that helped the Normans conquer England was the special training of their warriors on horseback. At this time, horses were so expensive that if an English fighter had one he would ride to the battlefield, but fight on foot. Fighting on horseback might have given him some extra height for throwing his spear and thrusting his sword, but it wouldn't have made enough difference to risk a valuable horse.

But Norman warriors had developed a highly effective new technique. Holding their spears firmly under their arms, they rode straight at their enemies, delivering a devastating blow with all the weight of the horse and rider behind it. This new tactic changed the course of battles, and transformed the way wars were fought for the next 500 years.

Battle gear

As well as specially strengthened spears, known as *lances*, knights also fought with swords, axes and clubs known as *maces*. They fended off enemy blows using big shields.

For extra protection, knights wore helmets, reinforced shirts and sometimes special guards for their arms and legs. They were also trained to fight on foot, as well as on horseback.

This is a painting from around 1250. It shows a knight on horseback wounding another knight with his lance.

All the knights shown here are wearing protective clothing known as chain mail. It was made by linking many small iron rings.

Noble fighters

The men who fought like this quickly took on almost legendary status. The awe-struck English called them *knights*. At first, any man who could afford a horse and put in the training could be made a knight. But soon knights started being chosen mainly from the families of other knights. These families were known as the *nobility*, because they were supposed to have *noble* qualities of bravery and loyalty. Before long, almost all noble boys became knights as the first step of their careers – even if they went on to become lords, bishops or kings later.

As well as fighting, knights had a vital role in running the country too. The king trusted them above everyone else. He chose his most important knights to become lords and officials, and divided up his land between them. In return, they promised to keep the peace in their areas, to help to run the law courts, and to fight for the king for part of each year, bringing plenty of knights with them.

In turn, the lords then divided up their lands among their knights, who promised to fight for their lord and guard his castles for part of each year. In England, the Normans started to put this system in place soon after William was crowned.

Training

Boys started training to be knights from a young age – sometimes as early as age seven. First of all, a boy became a *page*, and was sent to live with the family of a famous knight. He fetched, carried and learned about horses.

Next, he became a knight's personal assistant, or *squire*. He took care of the knight's battle gear, and learned how to handle weapons for himself.

Finally, if he did well, he was made a knight at a special ceremony. The king or another famous knight tapped him with a glove or sword and gave him a sword and other gifts.

It's not certain exactly what happened, but some claimed that William's troops had destroyed everything in their path – houses, crops and animals – while the terrified locals fled, dying in their thousands from starvation and cold.

Lords and castles

Even once he'd been crowned King of England, William couldn't relax. For the next five years, his army was constantly on the move, trying to keep on top of rebellions that erupted up and down the country – some of them even led by disgruntled Norman lords.

At first, William told English lords and church leaders that they could keep their titles and lands if they swore to be loyal to him. But many of them kept on attacking the Normans and William soon realized that he couldn't trust them to keep their word.

The new order

By 1086, there were very few English lords left – William had replaced almost all of them with his own men. The land was now divided up between Norman lords, each with his own knights and soldiers to help keep the peace in his area – by force if necessary.

They had a great new invention to help them: the castle. The Normans began building castles as soon as they arrived in England.

In this picture, the massive stone tower of a new Norman castle is being built. Norman stonemasons are in charge, but the fetching and carrying is done by English workers.

Stonemasons work in shelters known as lodges.

Stone is brought by cart from local quarries.

Mixing mortar

Castle building

The earliest castles were simple structures of wood and earth, designed to give fighting troops shelter and good views of approaching enemies. But, soon, stronger, more permanent castles were springing up all over the country. They were intended to keep the new Norman lords, their knights and their followers safe as they tried to impose their rule.

Castles could be spectacular, with vast courtyards enclosed by thick walls, and massive stone towers that housed huge halls for feasting, many bedrooms, toilets and even running water. They were status symbols as well as a safe places. Big and small, wood and stone, castles continued to be built all through the Middle Ages. But everyone building a castle had to get special permission from the King before they started.

Motte and bailey

The Normans created many castles with massive earth mounds, known as *mottes*. Next to the mound was a fortified area, or *bailey*.

This type of castle is often known as a *motte and bailey*.

The walls have outer layers of carefully cut stone. The middle is filled in with rubble and mortar.

Borderlands

In 1066, the frontiers between England, Scotland and Wales weren't fixed, so territories in the border regions – or marches – often changed hands. But now that William had the English crown, he wanted to push out his frontiers and gain power over the people beyond. At that time, Wales was divided into five kingdoms, each ruled by a warrior prince. In Scotland, however, power was more centralized. Although King Malcolm III had less control over some parts of the country than others, he was far stronger than any of the Welsh princes.

Chepstow Castle, perched on a cliff above the Wye River, in Wales, was first built in 1067, by William Fitz Osbern. He played a key role in the Norman Conquest and, as Earl of Hereford, was one of William's marcher lords.

Marcher lords

As the most powerful ruler in Britain, William expected the King of Scotland and the Welsh princes to recognize him as their overlord. This meant they had to swear loyalty to him and provide him with money and soldiers, in return for his protection. Some were more cooperative than others. So, to defend his lands and keep the locals in check, William posted his most loyal and capable lords in the marches. He also gave these marcher lords powers most other lords weren't allowed: they could make laws, keep their own armies and build castles without asking him first.

Princes and kings

At the start of the Middle Ages, 'prince' was a title given to the ruler of a small kingdom, or principality. It was only later that the title of prince came to mean 'son of the king'.

14

Normanizing Wales

From the outset, William instructed the marcher lords near Wales to invade the lands of any disloyal Welsh princes and replace them with loyal Normans. The Normans extended their territories deep into Wales and built several castles, including Chepstow in the south, Rhuddlan in the north and Cardigan and Pembroke in the far west.

This didn't happen without a fight, although the Welsh weren't simply conquered by violence. In some places, the Normans brought their rule and their way of life to Wales by building towns and monasteries and encouraging settlers who were used to Norman ways to live there.

Canmore

To the north, King Malcolm III, also known as Malcolm Canmore, had taken advantage of the upheaval during the Harrying of the North to raid Cumbria and Northumbria. William decided to deal with Canmore personally. So, in 1072, he took an army and a fleet up to Scotland. The two kings met at Abernethy, where Canmore was forced to swear allegiance to William, and to hand over his son Duncan as a hostage.

After Canmore's death, the frontier between England and Scotland was officially set for the first time, though this didn't stop further Scottish raids into England. At the same time, the Scots court came under more Norman influence, as Canmore's sons married English women and English replaced Gaelic as the language of government.

English exiles

During the Norman Conquest, many English nobles took refuge in Wales and Scotland. Among them was Edward the Confessor's great-niece Margaret, who married Malcolm Canmore. Scholarly and devout, she set up an abbey at Dunfermline, and was later made a saint.

Map of 11th century Britain

🏰 Marcher lordships

🏰 Early Norman castles in Wales

SCOTLAND

• Abernethy

Northumbria

🏰 Newcastle
Cumbria 🏰 Durham

ENGLAND

Rhuddlan
🏰 🏰 Chester
🏰 Shrewsbury
WALES
🏰 Hereford
🏰 Cardigan
Pembroke 🏰 🏰 Chepstow
Cardiff

This is the Domesday Book. It contains very detailed information about who owned what at the time of the Conquest.

Domesday

"He had everything investigated so thoroughly that there was not one single yard of land nor one cow or pig that was left out."

An entry about William's Domesday survey in the *Anglo-Saxon Chronicle*, a record of events written by medieval English monks.

One of the main reasons William had for taking over England was the country's wealth. He knew that the English kings had very efficient systems for collecting taxes. Now that he was in charge, William wanted to find out exactly who owned what, and how much they might owe him.

So, he sent out officials to every county in the kingdom, to put together a new and more thorough record, to make sure all of the facts were absolutely accurate and up-to-date. All the information was written down carefully, and then copied out into a great book.

Understandably, the English were very alarmed at such a detailed enquiry into their land being made by a hostile King. It felt to them like having their souls weighed up on Judgement Day, so they called the book *Domesday*.

Lords of the land

But although the Normans now owned the land, they left many English systems in place. For example, tax collecting and the law courts carried on much the same, and most English people continued to live as they had before 1066.

At this time, 90% of people were peasants, who lived in the countryside and raised crops and animals for a living. Different peasants had different arrangements with their landlords – some were free, meaning they could come and go as they liked and choose who they wanted to work for. But most peasants had to stay in the place where they were born and work for whoever owned the land for a few days each week. There were also some slaves, who had very few rights at all.

Most peasants continued to rent their land from a lord, or to work for him on his land, just as they had done before 1066. Everyone also continued to hand over a tenth (or *tithe*) of their produce to the Church, and to pay taxes to the King. This enabled the King, his lords and religious leaders to live in comfort and devote their free time to fighting wars, managing the Church and running the country.

Difficult times

But the Norman lords had come to England to get rich. So, they could be harsh landlords, demanding more from their peasants than ever before. Some peasants could barely afford these extra payments, while others, who had never had to work on their lords' land before, were suddenly made to do so.

For slaves, though, life became better. By 1100, the Normans made most slaves into normal peasants, who had to stay on their land, but had more rights.

Country life

Life in a medieval village could be hard. Peasants worked in the fields from dawn till dusk whenever there was work to do. Diseases and bad weather could wipe out their crops, and even in good years it could be hard to store up enough food to last through the winter.

But many medieval villages were well organized, to help everyone to make the most of the land. There were a few streets lined with houses, each with a small garden for growing fruit and vegetables.

Some nearby woodland was set aside for gathering firewood and some grassy areas were left for putting sheep and cattle out to graze. There were also two or three large fields around the village for growing crops. These fields were divided up again to form many strips, and each peasant had a few strips to farm.

In the Middle Ages, bread was the most important food. Well-off people ate fine white bread made from wheat flour, while poorer people ate coarser bread made from less expensive grains such as barley, or even from ground beans.

A mill was essential for grinding grain into flour. Around the time of the Conquest, people used the power of fast-flowing streams to turn their mills. But by around 1180, windmills like this one were being built.

Mills were expensive, so only landlords could afford to build them. They charged the local peasants to use the mill, and millers often made fat profits.

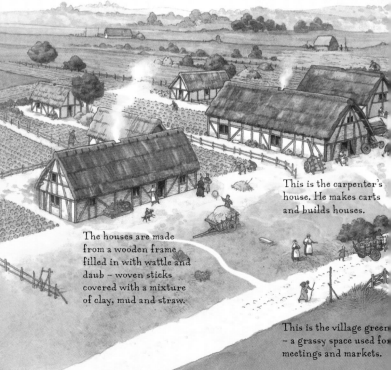

This is the carpenter's house. He makes carts and builds houses.

The houses are made from a wooden frame filled in with wattle and daub – woven sticks covered with a mixture of clay, mud and straw.

This is the village green – a grassy space used for meetings and markets.

The strips were allotted carefully, so that no one peasant had all good ones or all bad ones. Everyone agreed what to plant in each field each year – usually wheat or barley. They often left one field bare, so it would be more fertile the following year. And they sold any extra produce at local markets, to earn some money.

Not everyone spent their time growing crops. Often, the villagers appointed someone to care for all the sheep, pigs or cattle. Some peasants were carpenters, blacksmiths or cloth weavers, who sold their goods and services to the other peasants. So, even though they had to give part of their produce, their time and their money to their landlords and pay Church tithes, some peasants did well, and even became quite rich.

This scene shows a medieval village surrounded by fields. Peasants spent most of their lives in villages like these, but they did visit markets in nearby towns or villages.

Everyone grinds their grain into flour at this watermill, built by the landlord.

Beehives

Shepherd

Blacksmith

Vegetable patch

Church

This barn is for collecting all the produce paid to the Church as tithes.

Money lending

During the Middle Ages, many Christians believed they shouldn't profit by lending money. So they borrowed money from Jewish merchants, who were allowed to do this.

William the Conqueror encouraged Jewish merchants to settle in England, to help build up trade and wealth.

This painting of an English town was made around 1320-40. You can see the town walls enclosing houses and a large church. The poles sticking up from some of the houses are trade signs, to show everyone what kind of goods are sold there.

Towns and trade

When the Normans took over, there were only about a hundred towns in England, and by today's standards, they were very small. But they were growing in size and number. People from the countryside brought their surplus produce to town to sell at markets, and some moved into the towns permanently to learn trades or to work as servants for rich merchants.

As towns grew, trade also flourished. Markets boosted dealings in all kinds of goods, from grain and animals to dairy produce and salt. Craftsmen set up workshops to make and sell everything from bread to cooking pots, shoes, cloth, tools and ornaments.

Many newcomers had a better life in towns than they would have had in the countryside. The lords who owned the land where towns were built did well too. They charged the townspeople rent and collected their own fees on the goods sold at markets.

Trading places

By far the biggest town at this time was London. Its docks heaved with merchant ships coming and going. Many smaller towns held a special market, or *fair*, once a year to attract traders from near and far.

The Normans had many contacts in northern Europe, particularly in France, which was a source of goods such as wine. Other luxuries that couldn't be made in England, such as fine cloth and top-quality metalware, were shipped in. In turn, English merchants exported goods such as tin and most of all, wool, to the Continent.

But towns also had their downsides. Some traders tried to maximize their profits by selling shoddy wares or tampering with their weights and measures. And in many towns overcrowding, overflowing waste, house fires and thieves made life dangerous and unpleasant for everyone.

Making the rules

To try to keep things fair, clean and safe, important citizens banded together to set rules for their towns. Some formed trade associations, or *guilds*, and set standards for goods and trading.

Others set up town councils with mayors to organize market tolls, local law courts and repair and building work.

And others founded hospitals or charities known as *confraternities*, to take care of the poor and the sick.

Anarchy

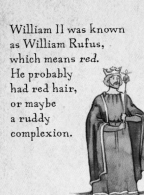

William II was known as William Rufus, which means *red*. He probably had red hair, or maybe a ruddy complexion.

In 1087, William the Conqueror died and his territories were divided among his sons. Robert, the eldest, became Duke of Normandy. The middle son, William, became King of England. But there was no land left for the youngest son, Henry. This division wasn't popular with anyone. Robert and William fought constantly over each others' land, and Henry often joined in, too.

Then, in 1100, William II died after a hunting accident. Henry was with him at the time, and some experts wonder whether he had a hand in his brother's death. Either way, Henry was crowned King of England three days later. By 1106, he had defeated his brother Robert and become Duke of Normandy, too.

Heirless Henry

After that, King Henry settled down to a peaceful rule. But tragedy struck in 1120, when his son and heir was drowned in a shipwreck. Henry wanted his daughter Matilda to succeed him, so he made his nobles promise to accept her as their next ruler. Then he married her to a powerful French lord, Geoffrey of Anjou. But, Henry's nephew, Stephen – also a grandson of William the Conqueror – thought the throne should be his.

When Henry died in 1135, Stephen rushed to London and had himself crowned before Matilda had a chance. Once Stephen was officially King of England, many lords felt there was little they could do about it, even though they had promised to help Matilda. But she wasn't prepared to give up that easily.

Sensing that Stephen was in a weak position, the Welsh rose up against English settlers in Wales, while King David of Scotland invaded northern England and grabbed Northumbria.

Family line

This family tree shows how Stephen and Matilda were related to William the Conqueror.

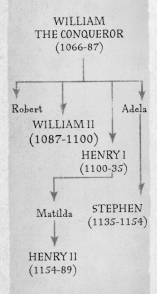

WILLIAM
THE CONQUEROR
(1066-87)

Robert   Adela

WILLIAM II
(1087-1100)

HENRY I
(1100-35)

Matilda   STEPHEN
(1135-1154)

HENRY II
(1154-89)

The dates show the years of each king's reign.

Cousins at war

Things really fell apart when Matilda and her forces landed in England to fight Stephen for the crown. They fought up and down the country, in Normandy and other parts of France. This bitter civil war lasted for most of Stephen's reign and is known as the Anarchy.

Sometimes Stephen had the upper hand, sometimes Matilda, but the ordinary people suffered most. Many were killed in the fighting, while others were forced to build castles for the opposing forces or were tortured for information. Thousands more died of starvation because no-one could grow or distribute food properly.

Finally, in 1148, Matilda retreated to France. It looked as if she had finally given up. But when Stephen's son and heir died in 1153, he realized that Matilda would win in the end. He signed a treaty leaving the crown of England to Matilda's son, Henry. Now at last there would be peace.

"And so it went on for nineteen years while Stephen was King...the land was laid waste and people said openly that Christ and his saints were asleep."

An entry about the Anarchy in the *Anglo-Saxon Chronicle*, a record of events written by medieval English monks.

During fighting at Lincoln, Stephen's forces were so desperate, they took over the cathedral as a base for attacking the castle opposite it. This photograph of Lincoln Cathedral is taken from the walls of the castle.

This is a medieval picture of Henry II.

Henry Plantagenet

Matilda's son Henry was already Duke of Normandy, Count of Anjou and Duke of Aquitaine when he became King Henry II of England in 1154. His vast realm stretched from the Scottish borders to the south of France, and later he would also count Ireland as part of his domain. Henry was arguably the most powerful monarch in Europe at that time, and he was determined to stay that way.

Taking control

Having come to the English throne out of a period of civil war, Henry's first task was to restore order and strengthen his authority. He earned the nickname 'Castle Breaker' because he had a number of castles pulled down, which had been built without royal permission during the Anarchy.

Henry considered himself to be the overlord of the rest of Britain. So he quickly set about reclaiming territory that the Scots and the Welsh had seized from the English during the turmoil of the civil war. King David's son, Malcolm IV of Scotland, reluctantly co-operated, returning Northumbria to English rule.

But the Welsh put up more of a fight. In 1163, Henry demanded that the Welsh princes recognize him as their overlord. Many refused, so he launched a massive invasion. It was a disaster. Despite having a far bigger army, the English knights struggled against heavy rains in hilly terrain, and were soon beaten into a retreat.

Into the Pale

Like Wales, medieval Ireland was divided into many small kingdoms. When one of the Irish kings appealed to Henry to help him put down a local rebellion, Henry sent over the English nobles who had been pushed out of Wales. Led by the Earl of Pembroke – nicknamed 'Strongbow' – the English knights soon crushed the rebels and began to colonize part of Ireland, which became known as the Pale. Realizing that they were becoming too independent, Henry sailed to Ireland in 1171, and made the English settlers swear loyalty to him. Many Irish kings joined them, but they didn't see Henry as their king.

The map shows:

London

English Channel

Rouen
NORMANDY
Paris
MAINE
BRITTANY
ANJOU
Chinon
POITOU
Poitiers
AQUITAINE
GASCONY

France in the 12th century

Land held by Henry II

Land under the control of the kings of France

The Anglo-French connection

Relations between Henry and Louis VII of France had been strained from the start. Henry married Eleanor of Aquitaine, Louis' ex-wife, and gained a huge area of central France as a result. In effect, he controlled more French land than Louis. As Louis was anxious to prevent him from gaining any more power, this often led to conflict between the two monarchs.

With so much territory to control and defend, Henry spent much of his 35-year reign on the move, crossing the English Channel as many as 28 times. London was the cornerstone of his empire, but the French cities of Rouen, Chinon and Poitiers served as regional capitals.

French was the language of government and nobility across Henry's empire. But many of his ordinary subjects spoke English, Gaelic and other different regional languages. Henry knew better than to impose foreign languages and customs on them. As long as they accepted his rule, they could live as they pleased.

"Now in England, now in Normandy, he must fly rather than travel by horse or ship."

King Louis VII of France was amazed at the speed with which Henry II moved around his empire.

Murder in the cathedral

One of the main ways Henry II enforced his rule in England was through the law. He reorganized the legal system and set up new courts around the country. He believed that, as King, he should have the final say in all matters of justice. But this led to an explosive row with the Church, and one man in particular: Thomas Becket.

Becket was the son of a wealthy London merchant. He was clever and ambitious, with a taste for the finer things in life. He rose to power at the royal court to become one of Henry's closest advisers, and even led military campaigns for the King. Then, in 1162, he was appointed Archbishop of Canterbury, the head of the Church in England. From then on, he ate only simple food and exchanged his expensive clothes for coarse robes. But the greatest change was in Becket's relationship with the King.

Taking sides

During the Middle Ages, almost everyone in England belonged to the Catholic Church, led by the Pope in Rome. So, Becket's loyalty was not only to Henry, but also to the Pope. The Church also had its own law courts, and when Henry tried to bring churchmen who had committed crimes to justice in his courts, Becket stood in his way. The dispute became more and more heated until Becket, fearing for his life, fled to France.

When Becket returned to England, he expelled from the Church all the bishops who had taken the King's side. It was the last straw for Henry. Exasperated, he raged, "Will no one rid me of this troublesome priest?" Four knights took him literally, and rode to Canterbury to execute the King's wishes. On December 29, 1170, they stormed the cathedral and murdered Becket.

By the book

A new set of laws that applied to the whole of England was produced during Henry's reign. At the time, the laws only applied to freemen – most peasants were still at the mercy of their lord.

Many lawyers now see this as the basis of today's English Common Law.

"There are two principles by which the world is ruled: the authority of priests and the royal power. The authority of priests is greater..."

Thomas Becket in a letter to Henry II, 1166

Saints and sinners

The murder caused an outcry, and the Pope declared Becket a saint. As penance for his part in the killing, Henry walked to Canterbury to visit Becket's tomb, wearing only a sackcloth, then he was flogged, naked, at the door of the cathedral. The King's humility won him forgiveness from the Pope and restored his reputation with the public. But the legal dispute was never resolved.

This is an illustration from an English manuscript from around 1200. It is one of the earliest surviving pictures of Thomas Becket's murder in the cathedral.

The Crusades

Henry II recovered quickly from the Becket affair. But the end of his reign was neither happy nor peaceful. He spent it fighting his sons Richard and John, who were both angry at the way he planned to split his territories between them when he died. And to complicate matters, in 1187, the Pope announced a Crusade.

Holy wars

Crusades were wars fought by European Christians against people who didn't follow the Catholic faith. The First Crusade started in 1095, when Pope Urban II urged western knights to drive out Muslims who lived in the Holy Land – the area of the Middle East where Jesus Christ had spent his life. But the Holy Land, and especially the city of Jerusalem, were holy places for Muslims too, so things were bound to become nasty.

The response to the Pope's call was overwhelming. Thousands of ordinary men, women and children as well as knights set off from all over Europe by land and sea. Many died of starvation, fatigue and disease along the way, and more were killed in fierce fighting when they got there. But, by sheer luck, one group of crusaders managed to capture Jerusalem in 1099.

Crusader king

In 1187, Jerusalem was retaken by the brilliant Muslim leader Salah al-Din – known to the crusaders as Saladin. The new Pope, Gregory VIII, called for another expedition, to regain Jerusalem. Although they were at loggerheads, King Henry and his son Richard agreed to join the Crusade. But before they set off, Henry died and Richard was crowned.

King Richard headed for Jerusalem right away. He and Saladin were both brilliant military leaders. They respected each others' abilities and almost managed to negotiate a truce. Meanwhile, Richard and his troops made great advances. But in 1192, news arrived that Richard's brother, John, had started a rebellion back in England. Richard knew England needed him.

A king's ransom

Richard's journey back home was a disaster. First, he was shipwrecked, then captured by Duke Leopold of Austria. The people of England had to pay a vast ransom to have Richard freed, and the country suffered for years after handing over a massive pile of silver. But Richard didn't enjoy his freedom for long. He went straight to France, to try to win back land the French had seized while he was away. And in 1199, during a siege, he was hit in the shoulder by an arrow, and died.

This 14th century manuscript painting shows a bloody battle between crusaders, on the right, and Muslim fighters.

Lionheart

King Richard was known as Richard the Lionheart. He was probably given this nickname because of his bravery. But one story told that he put his arm down a lion's throat and tore out its heart.

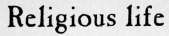

Religious life

The Catholic Church played a central part in daily life in medieval Britain. Most people went to church regularly, and their entire year was shaped by religious festivals that took place throughout the year. These included Easter in spring, Whitsun in summer, and Christmas in winter.

Men of the Church

The local priest was a vital member of every community. Priests had some land in the village fields, and collected tithes, so they were usually better off than the other villagers. As well as performing religious services, they were expected to look after the people in their area. They visited the elderly and the sick, and sometimes taught local boys.

Seeing is believing

A church was the social hub of the community as much as a place of worship – a meeting place where friends could catch up on the latest news. But walking into one could be an awe-inspiring experience. People believed that building a church was a way to praise God. So, the more elaborate and impressive, the better.

Church services were conducted in Latin, which most people didn't understand. In fact, many priests didn't have enough education to know what they were saying themselves. They simply learned the words by heart, then repeated them. So, the meaning of church services had to be communicated to the congregation in other ways. Churches were filled with beautiful paintings, sculptures and stained glass windows that illustrated important stories from the Bible.

Journey of faith

The furthest most people ever went from their homes was when they went on a spiritual journey, called a pilgrimage.

Pilgrims visited churches and holy places where saints were buried, or where holy objects called relics were kept.

Casket for Saint's remains

Pilgrims enter niches to pray

Many pilgrims brought back souvenirs, such as badges, as mementos of their trips.

30

This sculpture shows the Three Kings visiting the baby Jesus Christ and his mother, Mary. It is one of many alabaster (a kind of stone) sculptures that were produced near Nottingham and shipped all over Europe.

A church could choose from a selection of different scenes, or even slot several of them together in a wooden frame to make an impressive display.

Chantries

Some rich people paid for a chantry – a fund to pay for a priest or two to pray for the souls of the dead. These prayers were said at an altar in a parish church, or in a special small chapel built into the side of the church.

Spectacular services

To impress the congregation even more, the services themselves were filled with elaborate rituals, visual spectacles and inspiring music. Bells were rung at certain points to let people know that something particularly important was happening. The clergy wore richly woven and embroidered robes, and used beautiful objects, such as silver chalices, to give parishioners a sense of the grandeur and importance of the Church. A choir sang prayers set to music, as the congregation listened.

This photograph shows Merton College, part of Oxford University. The tower belongs to the chapel.

Scribes

Monks who produced hand-lettered manuscripts worked in a writing room known as a *scriptorium*. One monk working alone would have taken about a year to copy out the Bible.

Learning

There was a strong connection between education and the Church in medieval Britain. Some men dedicated their lives to religion by becoming monks, usually living apart from the rest of society in religious communities known as monasteries. Monks spent most of their time praying, working or studying, and lived by strict rules – they had to give up most of their possessions, ate plain food, avoided comfort and weren't allowed to marry.

During the Early Middle Ages, monasteries were the main places of learning, as monks preserved and copied out ancient texts handed down from ancient scholars. Their books, known as *manuscripts*, were hand-written and often richly illustrated, or *illuminated*. These books took a lot of work, so they were extremely valuable: a single book could be worth around the same as an entire field of wheat.

Wider knowledge

The first schools were set up to educate future monks and priests. There was a greater demand for educated parish priests, as people expected them to understand the Bible and to be able to preach sermons. Men seeking well-paid jobs outside the Church needed to know some Latin, too, to make legal records, or to keep accounts. Boys could get a basic education at elementary schools, called song schools, and soon all towns and a few villages had grammar schools which provided an advanced education in Latin.

Some boys went on to higher education. The universities of Oxford and Cambridge were established by the beginning of the thirteenth century, followed by one at St. Andrews in Scotland in 1413. Young men usually entered university when they were around fourteen years old, and studied for six years. They took lessons in subjects including philosophy, religious studies, geometry, algebra and music, to prepare them for careers in the Church.

But university graduates didn't just become parish priests or monks. They often found work as clerks, government officials, or school teachers, instead.

Going for gold

During the Middle Ages, a few men began conducting experiments into the natural sciences and *alchemy* – the science of turning lead, and other base metals, into more precious metals, such as gold. Among them, was a monk named Roger Bacon. Although he and his fellow alchemists never achieved their aim, they did make many discoveries about the properties of different metals. Bacon was also the first person to record making a rainbow by shining white light through glass.

Marvellous medicine

Doctors studied ancient Greek and Arabic medical texts about herbal remedies and other treatments. But some medicines worked better than others...

Doctors gave patients willow bark to treat fevers. This eventually led to the development of aspirin, a drug widely used today.

Leeches, a kind of blood-sucking worm, were used to draw blood from patients who were thought to have the wrong balance of fluids in the body.

Some unscrupulous doctors charged a fortune for medicines that might not work, by claiming that they included rare and expensive ingredients.

The first parliament

When Richard I died in 1199, he had no official heir, so his brother John became King of England. But King John seemed to do everything wrong. He lost some of England's territories in France, imposed harsh laws and taxes and accused his lords of plotting to overthrow him. He also angered the Pope, who cast him out of the Church and suspended all church services in England.

By 1214, the English lords had lost patience. They raised an army and cornered King John, asking him to sign an agreement limiting his power and giving them more say in government. It was known as *Magna Carta*, or the great charter. When John later tried to wriggle out of it, the lords hit back. In 1216 they invited Louis, the heir to the French throne, to London to take over. John fled and died a few weeks later.

The Great Council

With John dead, the English lords turned to his nine-year-old son, Henry, who was crowned in October 1216. Louis withdrew soon after. Because the King was so young, the lords had to help with government. But when Henry III came of age and took over for himself, the lords missed their power. They also grew uneasy that Henry's French wife and relatives were distracting him from English matters. They decided *Magna Carta* wasn't enough. So, in 1258, they demanded that Henry summon a Great Council of lords and bishops to help him decide all important matters.

Henry agreed, but he soon went back on his word and a civil war broke out. Simon de Montfort, Earl of Leicester, who was married to the King's sister, led the lords' forces. They rode to victory against the royal troops at the Battle of Lewes in 1264.

This is a copy of *Magna Carta*, made in 1225. Although King John revoked the document, most of his successors agreed to it. Many people today see *Magna Carta* as the first step on the road to democracy in Britain.

"No free man shall be arrested or imprisoned...or outlawed or exiled or victimized in any other way...except by the lawful judgement of his peers or by the law of the land."

Magna Carta, article 39

King in chains

Henry III was thrown in prison, and Earl Simon ruled in his place. To prove he had wide support, he called a Great Council of loyal followers, to back him up. For the first time in the Great Council's history, Earl Simon included wealthy townsmen and knights as well as bishops and lords. Never before had non-nobles been involved in government. This marked the origin of the House of Commons.

But Edward, the King's son, came to his father's aid. He raised an army in the Welsh marches and in 1265, defeated the lords at the Battle of Evesham, where Earl Simon was killed. Henry III was back on the throne, and was later succeeded by his son.

Edward I was careful to show his respect for the terms of *Magna Carta* and continued to consult the Great Council. In 1295, he summoned the biggest council ever, made up of barons, clergy, knights and townspeople. It later became known as the Model Parliament – England's first parliament.

Talking shop

The word *parliament* comes from the French word for *talking*. It meant a gathering to talk about important issues. Now, Parliament is the place where Britain's House of Commons and House of Lords meet to discuss things.

This illustration from a 16th century manuscript shows Edward I in the Model Parliament. King Alexander of Scotland is seated to the left of the throne and Prince Llywelyn of Wales on the right. On the outside are bishops, clergy and townspeople.

Law of the land

Edward I was a crafty ruler. He was careful to be seen to consult Parliament, but he often ignored its advice. And though he reformed many laws to make them less complicated, he advanced his own interests, too.

In 1274, Edward set up an enquiry into who owned what land, and how the country was being run. It was partly designed to make the law clearer, and partly to check up on dishonest officials. But the King's main motive was to discover how much land and power he could claim back from his lords, who he believed had illegally taken land rights from him. He also set up heavy taxes to pay for his wars at home and overseas. Meanwhile, Edward had set his sights on other prizes.

The Welsh princes

There had been tensions in Wales ever since the Norman Conquest. The Welsh princes – leaders of the different regions of Wales – were supposed to swear loyalty to the English king. But by the time Edward I came to the throne, one Welsh prince had become more powerful than the rest. Llywelyn ap Gruffydd (say Griffith) had taken the title Prince of Wales.

Profit and persecution

Edward also profited by persecuting Jewish merchants and their families, who had been in England lending money to people since the Conquest.

In 1275, he forbade all Jews from making a profit by money-lending, and in 1290 he expelled them from the country, seizing their land and property.

This is Beaumaris Castle. Edward ordered it to be built on the strategically important island of Anglesey in North Wales in 1295, as part of his total conquest of Wales.

Stubborn resistance

Llywelyn steadfastly refused to swear loyalty to Edward and even invaded English territory. So, in 1277 Edward led over 15,000 men to North Wales, Llywelyn's home ground. This show of strength convinced Llywelyn to sign a peace treaty. This treaty stripped him of many of his lands, but still left him as Prince of Wales.

But in 1282, Llywelyn's brother, Dafydd led a full-scale uprising in Wales. This time, Edward set off not just to invade Wales, but to conquer it completely. There was fierce fighting as Edward's army advanced against the Welsh forces, but the English had the upper hand. Llywelyn was killed in battle and the Welsh surrendered. Dafydd was later captured and executed.

In 1284, Wales officially became part of England, and many Welsh laws were replaced by English ones. Edward left workmen building a series of fine stone castles to defend his newly-won territory.

But the Welsh had still not given up. In 1294, there was yet another uprising, led by the Welsh people themselves. Once again, the fighting was fierce, but by 1295, Edward had triumphed – in Wales at least.

This medieval English manuscript shows Llywelyn ap Gruffydd meeting his death at English hands. No one knows exactly how Llywelyn died – some accounts say he was tricked by the English; others that he fell in battle, fighting bravely.

Unlike the Welsh, the Scots had managed to get along with the English relatively peacefully. But in 1286, King Alexander III of Scotland died in a riding accident. Four years later, his only heir, his infant granddaughter Margaret, died too. This left Scotland with no clear heir to the throne, and set off a chain of events that led to war between the two nations.

Taking control

A number of lords stepped up to claim power, but there were two leading contenders: Robert Bruce and John Balliol. To avoid a civil war, the Scots asked Edward I to help them to decide whose claim was the strongest. Edward chose Balliol, but only after Balliol had promised to recognize the English King as his overlord.

But, as soon as Balliol was crowned, Edward began demanding money and soldiers, and interfering in Scottish legal cases. The Scots were furious. In 1295, they made a treaty with France to help them throw Edward off. It was the start of the 'auld alliance' – a long-standing friendship between Scotland and France.

Fighting for Scotland

The English took it as a declaration of war and invaded Scotland in 1296. Edward's armies laid waste to southern Scotland. Balliol was forced to surrender, stripped of his crown and taken prisoner. Edward's message was clear: he wanted Scotland to be ruled by England from now on.

But the following year, the Scots rebelled. Led by a nobleman named William Wallace, Scottish forces defeated the English at the Battle of Stirling Bridge.

The Stone of Destiny

In 1296, Edward I seized John Balliol's crown and the Stone of Destiny, on which Scottish kings had been crowned since the 9th century, and took them to London.

The stone was housed in a specially built throne in Westminster Abbey. All English (then, after 1603, British) monarchs have been crowned on the throne ever since.

In 1950, a group of students stole the stone and took it to Scotland, but it was soon found and returned to Westminster.

In 1996, the stone was returned to Scotland. It's now on display in Edinburgh Castle.

In 1298, Edward invaded again, beating the Scots at Falkirk. For the next few years, Edward mounted attacks every summer, gradually wearing down his opponents. In 1304, the Scottish nobles finally accepted defeat. Only Wallace refused, but he was captured, taken to Westminster and hanged.

Bruce and Bannockburn

But Scottish independence didn't die with Wallace. In 1306, Robert Bruce, the grandson of the earlier Robert Bruce, was crowned King of Scotland, and launched attacks on the English in Scotland. The following spring, Edward I died. His son, Edward II, didn't pick up the fight straight away. This gave Bruce time to build up support and retake much of Scotland.

By 1314, Edward II could no longer ignore the threat. He led a huge army to Scotland and the two forces met in June at the Battle of Bannockburn. Against the odds, it was a major victory for Bruce, but it wasn't until 1328, that the English finally recognized Bruce's kingship and Scotland's independence.

This is a picture, from 1327, of the Battle of Bannockburn.

The English knights far outnumbered the Scots, who mostly fought on foot. But the Scots won, partly because the battlefield was boggy, which made the fighting extremely difficult for the English horsemen.

"Lay the proud usurpers low!
Tyrants fall with every foe!
Liberty's in every blow!
Let us do, or die!"

In his 1794 poem, *Scots Wha Hae*, Robert Burns imagines Robert Bruce addressing his men before the Battle of Bannockburn.

French knights line up
to charge at the English.

French armies had many
knights. They relied
on powerful cavalry
charges to win battles.

Fighting France

In 1327, Edward II was deposed and killed by
his wife, Queen Isabella. Their 14-year-old son
was crowned King Edward III. For a few years,
Isabella was in charge, but at the age of 17, the
ambitious Edward locked up his mother and
began to rule for himself. Determined to prove
himself a stronger ruler than his father, he invaded
Scotland, in an attempt to reconquer the country. He
soon defeated Bruce's successor, David II, then he
turned to France.

The French throne

Soon after Edward's coronation, King Charles IV
of France had died, and was succeeded by his cousin,
Philip. But Edward's mother Isabella was Charles's
sister, and Edward thought that, as Charles's nephew,
he had a better claim to the French throne than Philip.

In 1340, war broke out, and Edward openly claimed
the crown of France for himself and his heirs. The first
big battle was at sea, near the town of Sluys. The
English won, gaining control of the English Channel,
and the rest of the war was fought on French soil.

Lions and lilies

When Edward III
claimed the throne of
France, he changed his
royal coat of arms. He
added the French *fleur-
de-lys* – lily flower –
to the three
lions of
England.

Great victories

Edward soon proved himself a brilliant general. At the Battle of Crécy in 1346, his troops won a great victory. His son, the Black Prince, was just as successful. At the Battle of Poitiers, he even captured King John of France, Philip's successor. In 1360, the French had to sign the Treaty of Bretigny, giving up more than a quarter of their land to the English. Edward died in 1377, but the war wasn't over. Fighting continued, on and off, for the next 76 years, and the conflict is now known as the Hundred Years' War.

Secret weapon

Most of Edward's army was made up of longbowmen. Longbows could shoot arrows faster, and were easier to carry, than the heavy crossbows used by French archers.

Crécy

At the Battle of Crécy, Edward III used his longbowmen to devastating effect. Here you can see what happened.

🛡 English longbowmen   🛡 French crossbowmen
🛡 English knights   🛡 French knights

1. At the start of the battle, Edward arranged his soldiers at the top of a hill. They were outnumbered, but had a better position.

2. Philip commanded his crossbowmen to advance and fire, but they were beaten back by the English longbowmen.

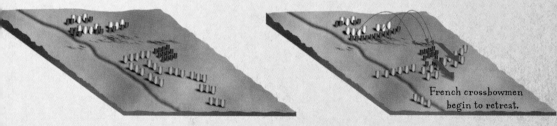

French crossbowmen begin to retreat.

3. The French knights charged over their own crossbowmen. English longbowmen rained arrows on the knights, halting the attack.

4. Some French knights reached the English battle line, but they were defeated by English knights on foot. The rest of Philip's army fled.

French knights retreat.

This is a painting from France, showing a mass burial of Plague victims.

Mystery illness

Even today, experts disagree about what caused the Plague. Most think that it was carried by fleas that lived on rats and bit humans.

Rats were a constant problem in the Middle Ages. Many people owned cats, but they still couldn't get rid of all the rats.

Plague

In the late 1340s, a terrible plague swept out of Asia and into Europe, wiping out nearly half the population. It arrived in Britain in 1348, and spread through the land with terrifying speed. The first signs were a high fever and black, foul-smelling boils – at first on the armpits, groin and neck, and then all over the body. Usually, victims died within 48 hours – but sometimes they dropped dead within minutes.

The wrath of God

No one knew what had caused the Plague, or how to cure it. Most people believed it was a punishment from God, and that the only way they could be saved was by praying. Meanwhile, the graveyards filled up, and bodies were piled in long trenches. By the time it died down in 1349, the Plague had killed more than a third of the people of Britain. Over the next 30 years, there were several smaller outbreaks, killing many more.

Aftermath

The Plague had a big impact on those who survived. Some lost their faith in the Church, as many priests had died of the Plague, and some people thought this showed that God was punishing them. But many people became more religious. They gained some comfort from joining together in brotherhoods to worship particular saints, and marching through the streets in processions to show their faith.

Peasant problems

With so many dead, it was difficult to produce enough food, as there were few peasants left to work in the fields. Landlords needed all the help they could get, but some peasants tried to use the opportunity to demand better terms, or even ran away to find land and work elsewhere. So the landlords clamped down, forcing their peasants to work under the old conditions. This only made things worse.

The Statute of Labourers

There was also a terrible shortage of other types of workers. Surviving workers demanded more pay because they knew their employers were desperate, and some left their jobs to find better ones. In England, Edward III worried that this might lead to the breakdown of order. So in 1351, he introduced the Statute of Labourers, which limited wages to pre-Plague levels and tried to prevent workers from leaving their employers. But it wasn't enough. Soon, growing discontent among the poorest people would lead to bloodshed.

Perpendicular architecture

After the Plague, a new, simpler style of religious architecture developed in England, known as *Perpendicular*. Some experts think the Plague caused the change in style – either because many masons died and new ones took over, or because religious ideas were changing.

This is King's College Chapel in Cambridge, built in the Perpendicular style. You can see the strong, straight lines that gave the style its name.

John of Gaunt

John of Gaunt was the fourth son of Edward III.

Like his older brother, the Black Prince, John fought in the Hundred Years' War in France, but he won few victories.

While Edward lay dying, John took over the King's Council, effectively ruling the country. He won a reputation for bribery and corruption.

After the Peasants' Revolt, John left England to fight a war in Spain, leaving the 19-year-old Richard to rule England himself.

The Peasants' Revolt

In 1377, Edward III died. His son, the Black Prince, had died the year before, so the English crown passed to Edward's grandson, Richard II. The young King was only 10 years old at his coronation. Just four years later, he faced a terrifying crisis, which tested his courage to the limit.

For the first few years of his reign, England was effectively ruled by Richard's uncle, John of Gaunt. But he became very unpopular, especially when he introduced heavy taxes to pay for the war with France. In 1381, he brought in a poll tax, by which everyone paid the same amount, whether they were rich or poor. Most people were furious, and when officials tried to collect the tax, riots broke out all over the land. This was the start of a great uprising which became known as the Peasants' Revolt.

Wat Tyler

The Peasants' Revolt was sparked off by the poll tax, but there were bigger things at stake. For centuries, many people had felt that the social system in England was unfair. Now the poorest workers saw a chance to win their freedom. In Kent, a craftsman named Wat Tyler began gathering a huge crowd. His plan was to march on London, and demand that the King abolish the peasants' duties to their landlords.

When they arrived in London, Tyler's mob ran riot. They set fire to John of Gaunt's palace and killed the Archbishop of Canterbury. While many of King Richard's advisers panicked, the young King bravely agreed to meet the rebels and listen to their demands. At Smithfield, the 14-year-old King Richard II came face-to-face with Wat Tyler.

The end of the revolt

But while Richard and Tyler were talking, the Lord
Mayor of London drew his dagger and stabbed Tyler
to death. He said that he was protecting the King, but
it was more likely that he had planned to get rid of the
rebel leader. The peasants might have attacked, but
Richard turned to them, calling out, "I will be your
captain!" It was the most successful moment of his
reign. With Tyler dead, the peasants went home,
convinced that the King was on their side.

In fact, Richard did nothing to help them. The
leaders of the revolt were rounded up and executed.
But, in any case, life in Britain was gradually changing
in the wake of the Plague, as landowners were starting
to allow their peasants more and more freedom.

This picture tells the
story of Richard's
meeting with Tyler.
Richard appears twice
– in the foreground, he
is shown watching the
Lord Mayor strike Wat
Tyler, and on the right,
you can see him
addressing the mob.

It is unlikely that Tyler's
band would have been
anything like as well
equipped as they appear
in this picture.

This exquisite painting was probably made in England around 1395, and is in the new 'international' style of art. It was made for the King, Richard II and shows him kneeling in front of three saints. Richard is praying and looking up to the infant Jesus, his mother Mary and a group of angels.

Literature and art

All through the Middle Ages, British musicians, architects, artists and writers were busy creating songs, buildings, paintings, carvings and poems. Although they drew inspiration from local traditions, they often used styles and techniques that were popular throughout Europe.

By the 14th century, a polished style, full of intricate patterns, elegant postures and details copied carefully from nature, had developed across Europe. It's often known as International Gothic. British architects and painters were now producing works very similar to those painted hundreds of miles away, while writers were experimenting with stories and styles from many different countries, too.

Native tongues

Up to this time, most writing had been in Latin, which only a few educated people could understand. But now, writers all across Europe were starting to compose works in their own languages. In Britain, poets such as Geoffrey Chaucer wrote poems in English that included local characters and events. Chaucer's most famous poem, *The Canterbury Tales*, describes his journey with a rowdy group of pilgrims to visit the shrine of Saint Thomas Becket at Canterbury Cathedral.

Language and religion

But there was also a more serious side to writing in English. Ordinary people who didn't know any Latin could begin to understand what writers were saying. People soon realized what a huge impact this might have.

In 1382, a religious teacher at Oxford University named John Wycliffe decided that people didn't need priests to teach them about religion. He started to translate the Bible from Latin into English, so everyone would be able to understand it.

Church leaders were outraged, as they believed uneducated people should not be allowed to read the Bible and form their own opinions. They denounced Wycliffe and his ideas, and quickly clamped down on his followers, who were known as Lollards. Some of these rebels were even burned to death.

But, from this time on, British writers began to use English more and more often. And when an English Bible was eventually published in 1611, it was partly based on Wycliffe's work.

This picture of Geoffrey Chaucer was painted in the margin of a richly illustrated copy of *The Canterbury Tales* from around 1405.

Printing press

For most of the Middle Ages, books were copied by hand. But in 1440, a German named Johannes Gutenberg invented a way of fixing together tiny metal letters and printing them onto paper. He produced Europe's first printed books.

In 1476, William Caxton set up Britain's first printing press. One of the first books he printed was *The Canterbury Tales*.

Medieval women

Men were officially in charge in medieval Britain and held all the top jobs – from kings and bishops to knights, lawyers and even village officials. So it's all too easy to forget the varied and important roles women played. Most medieval women got married and had children. But they were expected to work as well. This meant very different things for different women.

Learned ladies

As the Middle Ages went on, more and more people learned to read and write, including many women. Reading was a great help to women running households and businesses. Women were also encouraged to read prayers and other religious writings.

Ladies of leisure?

At the top of the social scale, queens had a great deal of power and influence. They usually had their own land and income and ran their own households. Queens were often important patrons, paying writers and artists to create great works of art. They could intervene in international politics, sometimes in ways that didn't meet their husbands' approval.

Lower down the scale, noblewomen took an active part in running their husbands' households, advising their husbands and taking the lead at feasts and ceremonies. When their husbands were away, or if they died, noblewomen often took charge, organizing vast estates, important business deals and even warring armies.

This is a medieval painting showing a group of nuns led by their abbess, on the left. They are holding music books, which they would have sung from during worship.

Jobs for women

The wives and daughters of businessmen and craftsmen often had a very active role in the family business. They helped out in the workshop as skilled weavers, dyers, bakers, leatherworkers or even blacksmiths – whatever the family trade was. And if a craftsman died, his wife often took over the business and ran it herself.

Poorer women often found work as servants, as assistants for craftsmen, working on farms, driving carts or even mending roads. All these jobs allowed women to earn a living, but also gave them a chance to meet people – including future husbands.

If they married, women often gave up paid jobs and helped in their husbands' work instead. Looking after children, cooking, cleaning and helping on the farm or in the workshop was a full-time job. But resourceful housewives could still make extra money by selling ale they had brewed, or spinning thread to be made into cloth.

For better or worse

Women of all social classes who didn't want to marry could become nuns. Better-educated nuns often rose to become powerful abbessess, running their own nunneries. So, many women had skilled jobs and did very well for themselves. But others weren't so lucky. Many men resented successful women and tried to prevent them from earning a living, by excluding them from craft guilds, or paying them less than male workers. Some Church teachings also made women's lives difficult. And, sadly, some women suffered at the hands of cruel employers, husbands or fathers.

Real women

Christina of Markyate was born around 1100 in Cambridgeshire. Her parents forced her to marry, but she went into hiding and eventually became a nun at Markyate. She was so famous, a book was written about her.

Margaret Paston was the widow of a 15th century Norfolk landowner, who left his affairs in disarray. Her letters still survive, asking for gunpowder and arrows, to defend Caister Castle from 3,000 armed men who were trying to claim it.

Margery Kempe was a married woman who lived in King's Lynn from around 1373 to 1438. She had religious visions, and made pilgrimages to Rome, Spain, and Jerusalem, leaving her husband at home.

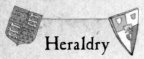
Knights' helmets covered their faces. This was confusing for anyone trying to work out who was who in a war or a mock battle. So knights started to display distinctive emblems on their shields and clothing.

Soon there were so many emblems, only specially trained men could remember which was whose. They were called *heralds* and the study of knightly emblems was known as *heraldry*.

Knights were proud of their emblems and passed them on to their sons and other family members. An English knight had this picture painted of himself with his wife, daughter and horse, all kitted out in his family emblems.

Noble pastimes

Among the nobility, women were considered important as an inspiration for men. People thought that loving a noble lady would inspire knights to be braver, more loyal and better-behaved. No one really knows how seriously most knights or ladies took this idea, but some certainly seem to have acted on it.

Some knights went on quests for adventure in the name of their lady-love. Others spent hours composing love-poetry, dancing and playing music to impress ladies – and other knights, too. But knights were also expected to fit in plenty of active pastimes, to keep them fit for fighting. Ladies were often involved in these activities, too.

Fighting for fun

Knights often fought in mock battles known as tournaments. In the early days, these could be bloody and chaotic, but rules were soon developed to stop them from killing each other, and knights started to wear special reinforced helmets and use blunted weapons.

Later tournaments often included a mock battle known as a *mêlée*, where two teams of knights fought each other in a designated area, under strict rules. One-to-one combats known as *jousts* were also popular at tournaments. Two knights charged at each other along a marked course. Points were awarded according to whether and where a knight managed to hit his opponent with his lance. A blow to the torso gained maximum points, while extra points were given to a knight who broke his rival's lance or knocked him off his horse.

50

This 15th century painting shows a joust between an English knight (on the left) and a French one.

The thrill of the chase

Hunting was another way for nobles to perfect their horseriding and weapon-handling, and there were many rituals involved. Noblemen were accompanied by servants whose job it was to find the prey and handle specially trained hunting dogs. Noblewomen often went too, but they sometimes watched rather than taking part. The most sought-after animals were reserved for nobles to hunt – strict laws forbade common people from catching the larger prey.

Different animals presented different challenges. Deer ran swiftly, so only the best dogs or archers could catch them. Wild boars weren't fast but they were strong and vicious, so hunters needed great timing and strength to spear them. After the hunt, the animals were taken home and eaten at great feasts.

Hawking

Women and men both joined in *hawking*, a type of hunting where specially trained birds of prey were used to track down and kill birds and animals such as partridges and hares.

51

Merrymaking

Noble people weren't the only ones who had fun – on festival days throughout the year, everyone from a peasant to a prince would join in the celebrations.

Many of these were Christian holidays that are still celebrated today. At Christmas time, people decorated their houses with greenery and mistletoe, and tucked into huge meals. Meat and fish of all kinds were eaten, and feasting went on until January 6, which marked the day the Three Kings visited Jesus Christ. Instead of Christmas presents, people exchanged New Year gifts.

Some festivals with pagan origins were also celebrated, though not always with the approval of the Church. May Day was a celebration of the fertility of the countryside, and at various times in June, summer games led to much drinking, dancing and feasting. In the countryside, bonfires were lit, and burning wheels were rolled down the hillsides, while Londoners decorated their houses with bright garlands of flowers.

During festivals such as midsummer, the social structure was turned upside down. A peasant was declared Lord for the day, and was treated like a noble by the other villagers.

Strange shows

On the feast of Corpus Christi, commemorating Jesus Christ's last day on Earth, guilds of craftsmen would put on plays based on Bible stories, performed in the open air around towns. The craftsmen made props to promote their trades, and no expense was spared on special effects. An audience could watch Saint John the Baptist being beheaded, and be splashed with ox blood in the process. Another play called for the actor playing Judas to hang himself from a tree – one actor took his role so seriously that he nearly died.

Extreme eating

Nobles celebrated special occasions with particularly lavish feasts. The dishes were elaborately prepared, with sauces made from expensive spices and dried fruits. Leftover food was handed out to the needy, and rich people sometimes invited a few poor people to eat with them. But there was more to a feast than just the food. Dancers and acrobats kept the guests entertained, and musicians played throughout the meal. Sometimes the arrival of a spectacular dish was announced with a trumpet fanfare.

In this medieval painting, peasants are celebrating May Day by dancing to bagpipe music and wearing green branches in their hats.

While Richard gave up the throne of England, there was a similar crisis in Scotland.

In 1402, Robert III's heir David was murdered by his power-hungry uncle. David's 12-year-old brother James had to flee the country.

But the ship was captured by pirates, and James was handed over to Henry IV of England.

James grew up in captivity, as the prisoner of the English King, while Scotland was ruled by his uncle. James took up the crown of Scotland in 1424, after marrying Joan Beaufort, the granddaughter of John of Gaunt.

The Welsh Prince

Ever since the Peasants' Revolt, Richard II's reign had gone downhill. He taxed the country heavily to pay for his lavish lifestyle, and heaped expensive gifts upon his friends. Meanwhile, he ignored Parliament, and made enemies among his most powerful nobles.

The usurper

Eventually Richard's cousin, Henry, Duke of Lancaster, led a rising against him. By this time, the King had lost all support. In 1399, he had to surrender the throne to his cousin, who became King Henry IV, the first Lancastrian king of England. Richard, meanwhile, was murdered in prison.

Unfortunately for Henry, he had no real claim to the throne. Richard's rightful heir was the Earl of March, the great grandson of Edward III. This made Henry a usurper. For his entire reign, he would face violent attempts to overthrow him.

Rebellion in Wales

Just one year after Henry took the throne, there was a major rebellion in Wales. It began as a dispute over land boundaries between a Welsh nobleman, Owain Glyndwr (say Glendower), and a marcher lord, Reginald de Grey. Henry sided with de Grey.

Furious, Glyndwr responded by sacking his rival's town, Ruthin. Before long, this local feud had become a full scale revolt against English rule. Welsh nobles flocked to join Glyndwr, and within a few months, they had proclaimed him Prince of Wales. The new Prince set about reclaiming Welsh lands from the English.

Hotspur

Henry's English enemies saw the Welsh revolt as a chance to overthrow him, and joined forces with Glyndwr. Among the rebels was a fearsome warrior, Henry Percy, or 'Hotspur' as he was nicknamed. Hotspur was the King's cousin, and had actually been in charge of putting down the rebellion – until he had switched sides.

At the Battle of Shrewsbury in 1403, Henry IV's army caught Hotspur on his way to join up with the Welsh rebels. It was a bloody victory for the King and his son, Prince Henry, and Hotspur was killed in the battle.

Glyndwr's rebellion continued for years after the Battle of Shrewsbury, but gradually the King's forces won the upper hand. Glyndwr was forced into hiding, and after 1412 he was never seen again. To many people in Wales he is a national hero, and the last true Welshman to claim the title of Prince of Wales.

"I can summon spirits from the vasty deep"

Glyndwr appears in William Shakespeare's play *Henry IV part I* as 'Glendower'. In this play, his is portrayed as a mysterious figure, who claims that he can perform magic.

These actors are dressed as Owain Glyndwr and one of his knights. The emblems on the flag and other kit were adopted by Glyndwr from the 13th century Welsh ruler Llywelyn ap Gruffydd. They are still used by the Prince of Wales today.

Fields of France

In 1413, Henry IV died. He had spent most of his reign fighting off attempts to overthrow him – but his son would become one of the most popular kings in English history. When Prince Henry became Henry V, he set up law courts to bring criminals to justice. This won him many supporters. He also pardoned his old enemy Glyndwr. Then he turned to France, renewing the war that Edward III had begun.

War with France

There had been a truce between England and France since the reign of Richard II, but Henry believed that he had a right to the French throne. He had proved his military genius in the fight against Glyndwr, and in 1415 he set sail for Normandy, with an army of around 12,000 men. The campaign began badly. Henry's forces were weakened by a bout of dysentery, and he decided to retreat to the port of Calais. But, before he got there, he came up against a vast French army, near the village of Agincourt. Some historians think there were 40,000 Frenchmen – outnumbering the English by four to one.

The Battle of Agincourt

Just as at Crécy and Poitiers, the French army included thousands of knights, while most of the English soldiers were longbowmen. Once again, this proved decisive. The ground was wet and muddy, and the French knights quickly got bogged down. The English showered them with arrows, slaughtering thousands. It was a triumph for Henry. After Agincourt, he conquered Normandy, and married the French King's daughter.

Henry's longbows

Just like Edward III, Henry V knew that archers armed with longbows could win him victory in battle.

Longbows were very difficult to use, and so archers began practising from boyhood.

Henry's archers were mostly peasants, and so their victories over the French knights were also seen as victories over their social superiors.

They were not all English, though – many were from Wales. The Welsh were famous for their longbowmen.

By law, all men in England had to train at archery regularly.

Defeat

But Henry's victories were short-lived. Two years after his marriage, the great warrior King died, leaving behind him an infant son, Henry VI, to rule England and France. At the same time, the French were growing more determined to drive the English out of their country. Gradually, they won back the lands that Henry V had taken from them, until the only territory left in English hands was the port of Calais.

After a long campaign, the final battle of the Hundred Years' War was fought at Castillon in 1453, when a French army, equipped with cannons, defeated the English. After this, the English gave up trying to conquer France altogether. They soon had far more to worry about at home, where trouble was brewing.

Joan of Arc

Joan of Arc was a French peasant girl who had visions of saints. She encouraged the French Dauphin (heir to the throne) to fight the English, and even led French armies to victory in several battles.

In 1430, Joan was captured by the English, and burned at the stake on charges of heresy. After her death, she became a French national hero, and was made a saint.

This 16th century painting shows Englishmen killing French prisoners after Agincourt.

These two soldiers are counting money stolen from their victims.

A family at war

Henry VI was just nine months old when he came to the throne, so England was ruled by a council of noblemen, who often argued among themselves. When the King was old enough to rule on his own, it soon became clear that he was not the great leader that his father had been. Henry VI was a gentle, religious man, who could not control his ambitious nobles. Worst of all, he suffered from bouts of insanity which left him unable to rule.

Wars of the Roses

The fighting between the Yorkists and the Lancastrians later became known as the Wars of the Roses. The Yorkists often wore the emblem of a white rose, while the Lancastrians wore a red rose.

York and Lancaster

During one of these bouts, Richard, Duke of York, was chosen to rule England until the King's recovery. But when Henry took back power, the powerful and popular Richard led an army against him, defeated him, and carried on ruling the country. Henry's wife, Margaret of Anjou, was furious. She was determined to win back power for her husband, and set about raising an army of her own.

So began a violent civil war to decide who would rule England. On one side was Henry's family, the House of Lancaster, led by Margaret of Anjou. On the other was Richard's family, the House of York. Both sides had good claims to the throne, for both Henry and Richard were descended from Edward III.

EDINBURGH

Hedgeley —
Moor 1464

Hexham —
1464

Towton
1461
● YORK

—Ferrybridge
1461

Blore Heath
1459
Wakefield
1460

Losecote
Field 1470

Ludford
— Bridge 1459

Mortimer's
Cross 1461

—Northampton 1460

—St. Albans 1455

Tewkesbury —
1471
Edgecote
Moor 1469
—St. Albans 1461
—Barnet 1471

● LONDON

Battlefields

This map shows the most important battles, and which side won.

 Lancastrian victory

 Yorkist victory

58

Edward IV

Battles were bloody, and power swung rapidly back and forth between the two families. At first the Yorkists won the advantage, capturing Henry and imprisoning him in the Tower of London. Then, at the Battle of Wakefield, they suffered a massive defeat and Richard himself was killed. His head was cut off and displayed in York, wearing a paper crown. But in 1461 Yorkists crowned Richard's son Edward IV. He finally defeated his enemies at the Battle of Towton, slaughtering thousands of Lancastrians.

The Kingmaker

Shortly after his victory, Edward fell out with his greatest ally, Richard Neville, the Earl of Warwick. Neville had earned the nickname 'the Kingmaker' for his help in putting Edward on the throne. Now Edward hoped to ignore his ally and make his own decisions.

Neville switched sides, forced Edward to flee the country, and restored Henry to the throne. But Edward refused to give up, and soon returned at the head of an army. At the Battle of Barnet, he defeated Neville's forces, and Neville himself was killed.

Peace

Edward was King again, and in 1471, it was announced that Henry had died in the Tower of London. For the next ten years the country was at peace. It seemed that the House of York had won, and that Edward's heirs would be the future kings of England. But it was not to be. When Edward died in 1483, his son and heir, Edward V, would be King for just two months.

Elizabeth Woodville

Edward IV married the beautiful Elizabeth Woodville in 1464.

At first, they kept their marriage secret, because Elizabeth was not from a noble family.

After the marriage was discovered, Elizabeth's relatives were given powerful positions in court. This angered Neville and many other nobles.

Under the Tudors,
Richard III was portrayed
as an evil usurper, and
Henry as the man who
saved England.

In the plays of the Tudor
playwright William
Shakespeare,
Richard is
a cruel,
hunchbacked
murderer with
no remorse.

"I am determined to
prove a villain."

A 16th century portrait of
Richard III. In the Tudor
period, it was changed to
make him look like a
hunchback.

The end of the line

Edward V was only 12 years old when he was
crowned, and everyone feared that war would break
out again. They were especially afraid that Elizabeth
Woodville's ambitious family would try to seize control.
In fact, it was not the Woodvilles who took power, but
Edward IV's brother, Richard, Duke of Gloucester.

Richard III

Edward IV had chosen his brother to act as the King's
protector, but Richard wanted the throne for himself.
He locked up the young Edward, and his 10-year-old
brother, the Duke of York, in the Tower of London.
Then he had himself crowned Richard III.

As soon as he became King, Richard began
executing his enemies without trial, and confiscating
land. Many people suspected that he'd had his two
nephews, the Princes in the Tower, murdered. When a
young Lancastrian from Wales, Henry Tudor, claimed
that the throne was rightfully his, both Lancastrian
and Yorkist nobles flocked to support him.
Everyone was anxious to be rid of Richard.

Invasion

Henry Tudor had been living in France, but in
1485 he crossed the English Channel with an
army, to take the crown by force. Many of
Richard's friends and allies deserted him, joining
Henry. The King's only hope lay with one
of the most powerful nobles in England,
Lord Stanley. But Stanley refused to
commit to either side, waiting to see
which army was likely to win.

60

Many soldiers at Bosworth carried poleaxes – heavy wooden poles with metal heads. Some experts think that Richard was killed by one of these.

The Battle of Bosworth

On the morning of August 22, 1485, Richard and Henry faced each other at the Battle of Bosworth. On Richard's standard was his personal emblem, a White Boar, while on Henry's was a Red Dragon, a symbol of his Welsh roots. Meanwhile, Stanley's troops stood on a hill above the battlefield, ready to join in when it was clear who would win. In the end, Stanley entered the battle on Henry's side, and Richard was killed in the fighting.

The victorious Henry Tudor was crowned Henry VII, and married Elizabeth of York, Edward IV's sister, finally bringing together York and Lancaster. After years of chaos and bloodshed, the fighting was at an end. Henry was the first of a new line of kings and queens – the Tudors.

Dodgy claim

Henry Tudor claimed he had a right to be King, as a great grandson of Edward III. But many people had closer links to the throne – including the Princes in the Tower.

Some historians even think it may have been Henry who had them killed, rather than Richard III.

To strengthen his position, Henry claimed to be descended from King Arthur.

Index

Acknowledgements

Every effort has been made to trace and acknowledge ownership of copyright. If any rights have been omitted, the publishers offer to rectify this in any future editions following notification. The publishers are grateful to the following individuals and organizations for their permission to reproduce material on the following pages: (t=top, b=bottom, l=left, r=right)

cover (background) © Bibliotheque Municipale, Dijon, France, The Bridgeman Art Library/ Getty Images, **(t)** Westminster Abbey, London, UK/Bridgeman, **(b)** Copyright 2006. Photo Pierpont Morgan Library/Art Resource/Scala, Florence.

p1 © British Library Board. All Rights Reserved/Bridgeman; **p2-3** © John Woodworth/LOOP IMAGES/Loop Images/Corbis; **p6-7 (t)** © akg-images/Erich Lessing/Musée de la Tapisserie; **p8-9** © Travelshots.com/Alamy; p10-11 Copyright 2006. Photo Pierpont Morgan Library/Art Resource/Scala, Florence; **p14 (t)** © Justin Kase zfourz/Alamy; **p16 (t)** © UPP/TopFoto; **p18 (l)** © British Library Board. All rights reserved, Add. 42130, f.158; **p20-21** © British Library Board. All Rights Reserved/Bridgeman; **p23** © Howard Taylor/Alamy; **p24** © British Library Board. All rights reserved, Royal 14 C. VII, f.9; **p27** Photo Scala Florence/HIP; **p29 (t)** Bibliotheque Nationale, Paris, France/Bridgeman; **p31** V& A Images/Victoria & Albert Museum; **p32 (t)** © Paul Watson/Travel Ink/Alamy; **p34 (tl)** © The National Archives/HIP/ TopFoto; **p35 (b)** The Royal Collection © 2008 Her Majesty Queen Elizabeth II; **p36-37** © David Lyons/Alamy; **p37 (tr)** © British Library Board. All rights reserved, Cotton Nero D. II, f.182; **p39 (t)** The Art Archive/British Library; **p42 (t)** Bibliotheque Royale de Belgique, Brussels, Belgium/Bridgeman, **(bl)** © British Library Board. All Rights Reserved/ Bridgeman; **p43 (br)** © Adam Woolfitt/Corbis; **p45** Photo Scala Florence/HIP; **p46 (t)** English or French, The Wilton Diptych © The National Gallery, London; **p47 (t)** Photo Scala Florence/HIP; **p48** © British Library Board. All rights reserved, Yates Thompson MS11 f. 6v; **p50 (b)** Photo Scala Florence/HIP; **p51 (t)** Private Collection/Bridgeman; **p52-53** Bibliothèque Nationale de France; **p55** © Green Bay Media Ltd; p57 Private Collection/Bridgeman; **p59 (r)** British Museum, London, UK/Bridgeman; **p60 (b)** Private Collection/Bridgeman; **p61 (t)** © Dick Clarke/Mayhem Photographics.

Additional editorial contribution by Rachel Firth
Additional illustrations by Dai Evans
Digital design by John Russell
Picture research by Ruth King